Strange Times

80 Lockdown poems

Jay Whittaker

Merinda D'Aprano

Julie Shaw

DEDICATION

With love to our partners, friends and families who shared the privations and the unexpected joys of those strange lockdown times. With fond memories of all those we met at a suitable social distance in parks and shops and streets. With immense gratitude to all those essential workers who did so much to keep us alive and fed and occupied throughout 2020 and 2021. And to our abundant and loving mother/father God be glory and praise for ever.

To Mum and Dad,
Christmas 2022,
with love
from Julie
x

ACKNOWLEDGMENTS

Jay, Merinda and Julie are immensely grateful for our dear and outrageously talented friend Nicola Rose, for allowing us to use her painting *I can see the Wind 1* as our cover illustration. Visit her website at https://nicolaroseartist.com for information on exhibitions, work in progress and work for sale.

TABLE OF CONTENTS

INTRODUCTION

When lockdown began, like everyone else, we had to grapple with how to cope with a changed world. For us, not being able to go physically to church was a huge blow: we felt bereft. Zoom services were a blessing, and for a short while we enjoyed Sunday Eucharists where the priest said the words of consecration and we all took bread and wine in our homes. The Church of England authorities quickly moved to ban this practice on what seemed to us spurious theological grounds, which was the stimulus for the first poem in this collection, Jay's *Eucharist in troubled times*, which he naturally shared with his wonderfully creative friends, Merinda and Julie. When it became clear that the three of us were all feeling creatively inspired in the strange circumstances that Covid thrust upon us, we set up a WhatsApp group which we called Poets' Corner. For much of the Spring and Summer of 2020 we wrote and wrote, tweaking and adapting our efforts in response to the others' incisively constructive critiques. This collection of poems is the result; after the initial creative outpourings of the first six months of the pandemic, we continued more sporadically up to the Spring of 2022, when most of the lockdown restrictions had been lifted.

BEGINNINGS

Eucharist in Troubled Times

We give you thanks and praise as we recall
the piercèd side, the gouging thorns, the flesh
exposed. Naked. Held to ridicule.
You do not shun the public place, the lash
of jeering words. Unshielded, there you hang
alone. Once, years before, a growing boy,
you startled and amazed the gathered throng
of elders – now, this brutal, bloody ploy
to keep their power and influence intact
means they can turn their backs. We meet your gaze
each time our gathered throng meets to enact
our sacrament. We give you thanks and praise
in broken bread, in many rooms or one,
needing no mandate save from God's own Son.

Jay

Strange Times

These are strange times, we say, say on repeat.
The strangeness of a lorry load of grief
while lorries pass in ones, their passing brief,
their purpose sanctioned and their journey meet.
Strange times, when silence heavy and tight lipped
leaves space for birdsong, bubbling with sound
while sunshine bursts its rays upon the ground
and we, fenced within rooms, feel our wings clipped.
What ease for grief, what remedy for loss?
A face, a voice, when we but long for touch?
We search our virtual worlds, we decathect,
we look for meaning still amidst the dross,
we hope, but hoping, hope for not too much
and shape strange lives round strange ways to connect.
Julie

Corona virus infects the church.

They marshalled God
Till god was small
And hardly any point at all
They claimed the power
Within one room,
And banished God from using Zoom.

In disbelief and shock and pain
Our loving communion felt the strain
Without the touch of God to gain
Would we ever need the church again?

But God the resurrecting power
Was all around us hour by hour
And spirit-filled we felt that grace
Regardless of the cyberspace.

Our God is greater than the tomb,
And bigger than the bishop's room,
And we the faithful, ever true
Know we feel God's presence too,
And share that presence in our heart
(Even the consecrated part).
For God has harnessed the inter-web
And by such means we all are fed.

A church is not a fortress cold
The amazing power of God to hold
It is a place for love to flow
A place where others come to know
The deep and everlasting Love
The Word and bidding of our God.

As Jesus said 'do this for me
Whenever you eat, in memory'
So in a building or on screen
Consecrated, lifted, seen,

Blessed by Christ our great high Priest,
He bids you welcome, come and feast.

Merinda

OCCASIONAL POEMS

Not surprisingly, given the glorious weather that came with the first 2020 lockdown, we all spent a lot of time outdoors, in our gardens or enjoying the periods of government sanctioned exercise we were allowed. Many of our poems reflect this.

Hiatus

Horizon to horizon, clear blue,
save for one feathery vapour scar,
the sky calls mutely, 'Please, forget me not,
but let me be. Give me this quiet time
to rest and heal.'
Still a distant drone of cars
(but fewer than before)
jars (but just sporadically)
against the tranquil madrigal
of blackbirds, sparrows, collared doves.
They trill and chirrup, coo and my
fractured soul begins to knit.
The fevered and the wheezing earth,
infected by the virus of our greed
may breathe a little easier a while;
a brief respite, not looked for but
much needed brings
a ghost of healing on the breeze.
Jay

The tree

The tree stood shining,
yellow with sunlight
through its amber leaves
and the warm burning red fringes.
Not a mustard tree
grown huge through the
magnificence of God's joy.
Not a fig tree, fecund
with juicy fruit
for sheltering birds
and sating our appetite.
Not a frankincense, myrrh or cassia,
no sweet bark or rising perfumes here,
no sacred shiver
and no holy smoke.
Not a majestic cedar
with purifying power.
But a small, humble
acer, set against the azure of the sky.
Bunches of keys are scarlet fruit.
Keys to the happiness
of blue tits,
of passing neighbours
and of my own hungry eye.
The charming beauty of this tree,
swaying with grace,
and ripples of the breeze,
resonates with the glory
of a greater kingdom.
If only we could remember to see it.
Merinda

The Rain

Shocking, cold, wet
unwelcome,
trickling and tickling

with icy fingers
seeping and soaking
Wetting the frogs' heads,
spilling the blossom,
drenching the scrapes
filling the ponds
slaking nature's thirst.
Teeming rain,
greening the plants
blackening the soil
greying the sky
and blurring the garden.
But buried seeds awaken
water-quickened,
rupturing
to new life.
Hallowed rain.
Merinda

Sleep

Sleep, my comforting friend, where have you laid
your potent head, and why have you left me?
The swelling hours are burgeoning and frayed,
stuffed with fear and wondering what will be,
all shrouded in the fearful dark of night
that lets the demons eat into the sense
that recognises folly in the light.
And so with teeth and reason clenched and tense
and gritted eyes that stare in scratchy blear,
I beg you friend to come and share my bed,
I cannot rest until you hold me near
and pull me from my circulating dread.
And only when I know that you are lost
ungraciously you steal to me at last.
Merinda

Daisies

In clumps and clusters on the lawn
with sorrel and with buttercup,
with red-green stalks and petalled ruffs,
and golden faces gazing up;

we have no pride, we seek no place
beside the rose or fleur-de-lys –
content, we flourish on the ground
and feed the friendly questing bees.

Some call us weeds, but we don't care.
Born of the earth, and of the one
whose course we track across the sky,
we are the children of the sun.

Jay

Musings on a park bench.

God of the wood chip, the leaf and the stone,
God of the cigarette butt –
innocent looking, beige-wrapped inch of poison –
God of the bottle top,
gaudy, red and gold,
crimped coronet with its own simple beauty.
God of the bluebottle, searching the earth,
for what? as it flits here and there,
wings of dark lace swept back.
God of the virus, elusive and feared,
God of the jade green paint on the bench,
and the pewter grey splodges
where paint's peeled away.
God of the unloved, unhuman, unknown.

Jay

Corrymeela

The Presbyter Ray Davey
counter of antipathy,
horrified by apathy
set up a community.

Rival to sectarian bombing
aimed at ultimately calming
raging troubles of the region
caused, and solved by our religion.

Corrymeela was the centre's name
and it welcomed warmly all who came,
from each Christian denomination
tribe, community and nation.

The spirit called the blessed members there
to poetry, advocacy, and prayer,
bringing us reconciled into God's hands
and spreading God's favour throughout the lands.

Their prayer deeply rooted in the croi,
for fifty-five years of courage so key
to sharing forgiveness and love of our God,
and promoting peace throughout the world.

Merinda

Seasons of mists

Seasons of mist
of harvest and share
of fruits and seeds and wind-swept hair
of all that has flourished in God's great care.
The golden sun
in an azure sky,
beauty that gladdens our jaded eye,
diversity money just could not buy...
and mellow fruitfulness.
But the dawning reality of the eco affair
shows us we need to be aware,
in though and intention, in action and prayer
protecting what the creator put there...
The food that we eat
the places we meet
our breath in the air
and the ground neath our feet.
The bounty our father and mother of love
handed to all so we would have enough.

So we scatter the seed and reap the land
and share what we have with a generous hand.
Unless meanness and greed
are the method we use,
so others are hungry while we have their food
and those who are labouring hard in the field,
who are working to feed us
cannot pay for the yield.
And as we consume
way beyond what we make,
do we even consider that we're on the take?
And the present from God
our planet so blue
and green and perfect,
are we ruining it too?
Smoking and steaming the clouds in the air
raining pollutants on, well, everywhere,

chopping down forests, clogging the sea
a selfish avoidable waste plastic spree.
And the creatures that swim and walk and fly
need protecting from you and I
as we trample across their habitat
building or using or baiting the trap.
But this season of harvest, fruit and gain
is time for us to think again.
The beauty of this earth is for us
and given so freely by our God,
the skies, the seas, the creatures, the trees,
all that our natural sense reveals.
Creation is now in its autumn dress
heavenly multicoloured excess,
so it's time to fix our devouring way
by loving this planet every day.
Our overwhelming glorious world
our creator's genius unfurled.
For beauty, and life, and joy and food
Great God we give you gratitude.
Merinda

Lockdown prayer - for forgiveness and empathy.

Lockdown hurray
a free holiday
with no need to commute
and the furlough will pay...

But I do feel a bit trapped, you hear me say,
when to you it's another imprisoning day –
just like all the others, with little respite
after each unforgiving endless night.
A body that batters you down with pain,
or screams with exhaustion again and again.

Or is it the place where you must live
with those who deliberately spurn your request
to see you as you do,
the person you are,
instead choosing to scorn you and call you bizarre.

Or is it your keepers who've trapped you within
a prison of kindness
by carer or kin,
who have made you conform,
'to help you,' they claim,
as they slam the door of your closet again.

So lockdown in fact
doesn't matter to you,
it is business as usual,
it is just what you do.
As I pray for the virus to go away
for you it may never be fully okay.
But you hold your tongue
and just agree.
You don't want to frighten, or embarrass me,
with grief that cannot be assuaged
or your self-destructive guilt and rage.

So I tell you of birdsong
of projects, of sun,
of poems, of cycling,
of gardening and fun,
new stuff that I've managed to find time to do
and you know I've spectacularly failed to see you.

Lockdown I say,
like a free holiday,
I'm lounging at home
on government pay...
But you are made fearful
your job might be lost
and your savings won't cover
the subsequent cost,
and the shame and anger
and tangible pain
you don't share with me
could just drive you insane.
So as we chant what 'will be will be'
you watch cracks appear in your sanity.
Our lives will be different,
that much is true,
but what's my mild frustration
demolishes you.
Lockdown, a trap,
for better or worse,
for me a great gift,
for you a dread curse.

O Christ,
give me eyes to see the cross
that others bear in pain and loss.
Forgive my foolish unconcern,
help me to understand and to learn,
so with wisdom and humility
I might respond with empathy.

Merinda

Grey cyclist

I'm not a lycra man-imal
I'm not a racing type at all
I'm just a fat old woman who
wants to ride her cycle too.
And so I set off down the road
a chunky bike
a heavy load.
My goal to get some exercise
to help my ailing joints to thrive,
and stay upon my trusty steed
as I coast along at moderate speed.
My panniers rattle
my ears get chilled
my soul in ex-cite-ment is thrilled..
The rushing wind glazes my teary eye
and I feel like a whale who can finally fly!
Iv'e got a yellow jacket
with the grey fluorescent strips,
and I always wear my helmet
even on the shorter trips.
I'm generally cautious
as I reach the carriageway,
with a willing wind behind me
I'll make excellent headway.

But oh the horrid bicycle lanes,
those broken strips around the drains
where ironworks stick above the 'mac
and every six inches a crack
or curb stone edge on the attack
to throw me off the given track
while grit and glass provide the spike
for puncturing my lovely bike.

And to my horror, the royal pain,
there are cars parked in the cycle lane,
so I swerve to the busy road again.
While cars race past

too close to call
almost causing me to fall
or rumble behind me,
and rev and hoot
and try to knock me off my route
and kindly signal as they roar by
two fingers up ,
'Oy grandma die.'

The path is broke,
the trees hang low,
the gutter is no place to go.
Around parked cars
or pavement breaks
a brave and dogged soul it takes.
And yet my stiff and aching knees
through exercise have found their ease,
and lungs and heart at lazy rest
by surging fitness have been blest,
and in the glorious open air
I lose my trapped indoors despair
and freedom is the rich reward
of cycling on the open road.

Although you might prefer to drive
I want us both to stay alive,
me on the gliding frame of steel
and you behind the motor's wheel.
So when you see me on the street,
a plump and improbable athlete
be kind, and do not go too fast:
consider the cyclist you're zooming past.

Merinda

Locked, early evening.

I sit, imprisoned in my erstwhile shelter
looking inward at the gathering gloom,
where the lamp illuminates
only the shadows and the corners
of my flickering, hovering dreads
and lonely room.

I sit, in the same old chair
with familiar vista of this confining space,
denying myself any trick or treat
but cooling, unwanted tea to drink.
I brood on how it all remains the same -
except the blooming of all that is bad
which grows steadily to fill the room
till I am too squeezed to think.

I sit. And I turn from the window on the frightening world.
I do not see the colours of the autumn leaves
the glistening rain upon verdant lawn
the gleam of bright morning or yellow evening sun.
No creatures catch my jaded eye.
The day, whatever the time, is done.

I sit, but do not see
the bouncing sparrows and chasing squirrels,
nor the fat pigeons on the
leaf-bedecked paths.
The fruit from the wet tree falls
gleaming with fresh droplets,
and will decay magnificently although I will fail to notice it.
Life, undeterred by my determination,
carries on unabated.
But it is warm with fear and fury here
and I am nestled in a stultifying womb,
unable yet to be born into the light of hope,
licking endlessly
at the cuts and scars
in my contorted imagination.

I sit, and comforting myself, remain as still as I can,
and wish to God I could move.

Merinda in response to visiting a friend

Rhythm (to be beaten, on a bodhrán perhaps)

Rashers and sausages
Rashers and sausages
Black and decker
Heartbeat.
Thump thump thump
Pickled onions
Londons burning
Pour on water
Touching the void
Dance in the kitchen
Jump in the kitchen sink
And... (click)
Rashers and sausages
Sailor's hornpipe
Let me in
Shine like a star
Slow to stop.

Merinda

The Dark Detox of the Soul

You think that you have come so far,
and done so well.
Time spent on Godly work? Tick!
A goodly gift of many golden hours.
Talents used, as all can tell? Tick!
Your strong, creative, much blessed soul
enriches all the fellowship.
Teacher of the truth? Tick!
Such clarity, such charity,
such style, such wise yet simple words.

Indeed you have come far, so far.
As far perhaps as from your door
to your front gate, with but a trek
around the world to go.
As far as the marathon's starting line,
the check-in desk, the booking page.

Do you not know what is required?
A purging of the poisons deep within,
the pride with talons in each cell,
the anger festering in your gut
the age-old grudges sapping at your strength.

Will you accept the surgeon's knife,
lie paralysed and terrified
while all your secret shames are brought to light?
Can you bear the purging of your pains,
the scourging of your buried fears,
the outing of your angers, lusts and hates?

Do you dare believe that angry you,
that twisted, deviant, tarnished, nasty you
is lovable, is loved?
Do you believe that tantrum throwing child,
that bullied bully, worthless worm,
is worth redeeming, worth a mother's love?

Don't dare to think I died for well-dressed you,
to keep your masquerade alive,
to save you from the crumbling of your pride.
I took the scourging and the piercing thorns,
the hammered nails, the drowning breaths,
and all for you:
you, the battered, broken child,
you, the shamed, self-loathing worm.

Will you dare brave my touch?
Allow my arms to wrap you to my heart,
my hands to gently salve your wounds,
and wipe your tears away,
my eyes to meet your fearful eyes?

I seek the true child cowering within:
that is the hell I dare to harrow,
that is my passion's quest.

Jay

The Ten Passive Aggressive Commandments.

1. Thine own interests outrank the other's.
2. Thou shalt not dwell on the other's soul.
3. Let no perceived slight pass unpunished.
4. Thine own space and time is sacrosanct, whatever the other's needs.
5. Thy birth family's customs are superior to the other's.
6. Thou shalt not let cherished grudges die.
7. Thy spite shall be for thy partner alone.
8. Thou shalt not take advice from do-gooders.
9. Thou shalt tell the exact truth: it is a powerful weapon.
10. Thou shalt wallow in bitterness rather than covet others' joy.

Jay

Collecting sticks

We walk in the cold woods
and pick up sticks.
Kindling for the fire
like peasants
watched by Good King Wenceslas

The sticks may well be damp,
but soon will dry
spread on the open hearth,
that makes a home.

We could have burned shop-bought shard and shim
or woolly bundles wrapping solid paraffin.
And yet,
like before in the chilly woods,
with grandad
such a time ago –
those long gone days
of childish glee:
we collect sticks
to get the fire alight.
The task itself
our cheerfulness ignites.
They always say
wood warms you twice.

Merinda

I can see the wind 1

The wind shark swoops and scythes in space
carrying carnage and cleansing in its wake,
beholden to none, constrained by none,
ancient elemental predator
of all that's neat and trim and staid.
Uprooter of forests
pillaging branches and leaves and seeds,
shaker of seas
summoning storms and waves and spray.
Itself, and no other, lulling its prey
as it basks and murmurs in summer shade,
then soars and howls till chaos reigns.

Jay (based on a painting by Nicola Rose)

On my Profession as a Franciscan Tertiary 27 2 21

When I am broken, overwrought with shame,
a tearful child, alone in angry pain,
you lift me up, and gently speak my name,
and gaze at me, and smile and say
that I'm your funny valentine,
that I am your delight,
that you need me and that I have been loved,
that you have been,
and always will be my friend;
that you made me,
and love me,
and will me to exist,
that at my soul's centre you, Lord,
choose to dwell,
that you brought me into your banqueting house,
and your banner over me is 'Love',
and when I sleep you watch me breathe,
and stand and gaze and love me,
and that you sorrow over my hurts,
and when I stray
you long to bring me home,
and bid me welcome,
and shoo away my doubts,
until I sit and eat
and rest in you.

Jay

Hypocrisy

Hypocrisy's an ugly trait, it is a hidden sin.
It wears an outward ring of truth that hides a rot within.
It's the bafflement of all that's good,
the just will feel despair:
for when you stare it in the face
sincerity's not there.

Hypocrisy, hypocrisy, there's nothing like hypocrisy,
it damages the moral law and leads us to depravity.
Superior deceitfulness will hide what's really true,
and swear that right is always wrong to get one over you.
You may know there is injustice
and you search, but be aware,
that when you open up the box
real honour isn't there.

It's like the lovely vicar who is warm and welcoming
then takes the opportunity to say your life's a sin,
though he has a secret boyfriend, his companion, Fr Jim,
but he keeps him in the closet, so the truth cannot hurt him.

It's when the politicians say they care about us all
but when it's food for starving kids they'll vote against the bill.
You can shout out with unfairness
you can shout out in despair
but hypocrisy is blatant, so
you haven't got a prayer.

Hypocrisy, hypocrisy, there's nothing like hypocrisy,
it's a lie in truthful shape
permitted by plain apathy.
It's concealed in whitened sepulchres
with rhetoric and rules
to hide the truth from prying eyes:
it takes us all for fools.

It's when the pious Christians
That hold the Bible high,

denounce your faith
And scorn your face and hang you out to dry.
They like to say they love you,
but don't be taken in,
for actually they're saying
hate the sinner; blame the sin.

Hypocrisy, hypocrisy we're calling out hypocrisy.
It'll fight you back with tooth and claw,
it likes the double-talk you see.
You shout the truth to power and expose the feet of clay
but when you show your evidence, you'll find they look away.
The truth is inconvenient, so covering a track
becomes the major business – shield the fibbers from attack.

Still, the Bishops are quite clear on this,
gay's not a way for living,
unless you stay in secret though –
of that they're more forgiving.
And some folk want to help us,
they only want to pray,
it's not conversion therapy
if it just shuts up a gay.

Hypocrisy, hypocrisy, why bother with hypocrisy?
Well, it could quite improve your lot
pretending to be who you're not -
with the facade of honesty
perpetuate the mockery.

So if you do a worser thing
be sure to keep it hidden.
You must be caught by witnesses.
for abuse to be forbidden.

Until the smell of rank deceit
is larger than the power seat,
when falsehoods can no longer cheat,
then it becomes something we can beat.

Integrity, integrity, our prayer is for integrity
the grace of God in human form
that brings the truth so blessedly.
It holds up kindly reason,
honest justice starts to shine,
and shouts to all who'll listen
that hypocrisy's a crime.

Merinda

world's edge

sitting at the world's edge
in a garden chair
'who do you look for?'
calls a wood pigeon

sky seems vast above
circus tent stretched tight
to its highest point
by the invisible pole of my perception
sloping low to each horizon
great dome above
sphere circling our hazelnut globe
but it is nothing
the stretch the slope the height the dome

dove rests fat on a branch –
awkward pollarded twisted tree
ugly forking leaf-encrusted rune
in black green silhouette against the sky

moss droppings litter
the time-stained paving stones

Jay

FOUR SARUM POEMS

Jay wrote the following four poems during visits to Sarum College in Salisbury as part of his training (following in Merinda's footsteps) to be a spiritual director. The second and third sprang from conversations with his friend, the Revd Rona Stuart-Bourne.

sacred space

space to stroll or sit
a sea of grass, punctuated
by sturdy, steady trees proclaiming life

the great Cathedral
rocksteady a millennium
quietly proclaiming God
claiming a space for God

the tea room
a bounded space
the railings marking out a courtyard
but gapped, open to welcome guests
in sacred hospitality
where spirit meets with spirit within Spirit

cosmic Space stretches far above
the imagined sky blue dome which veils
its boundless, unimaginable reach
diffracted light of day
rendering stars invisible

yet Space is not more sacred than
the gaps between the daisy's petals or
the thrumming, potent quantum space
that holds in place the skeleton and tissue
of the questing wasp

God is not of the gaps
but of the sacred spaces that connect

Sing in the face of death

Where (do you think)
  is my mother's spirit?'
  she asks,

herself a mother now,
  a dozen years past childhood, yet
  still her mother's child.

The jolt of loss
  tugs her back
  to half-forgotten streets

to playgrounds, sweet shops
  songs and meals
  her mother's arms.

The voice no longer there
  which all her life has marked
  her going out and coming in,

has lullabied and soothed
  and chided, challenged,
  blessed and reassured.

'Where,' she asks,
  'is her spirit? Is she still
  with me?'

How to explain?

How to be the voice
  that guides her in her tears
  to see the flecks and speckles that remain,

the love splashed on her life
  in myriad ways, in which
  the bone and marrow of her soul is steeped?

She will find strength,
  after the tears have cleansed
  her grief-clogged pores

to sing in the face of death,
  and as her song
  of firm enduring love

colours the desert sands
  with budding hope,
  an echo drifts across the dunes

the absent voice
  in harmony with hers
  breathes from wells of love

whispers that not one whit
  of spirit or of love
  is lost

Rocks in the stream

Rocks in the stream, remnants of ages past
when marauding torrents carved a river bed,
carrying off soil and plants and lighter stones,
leaving the hard recalcitrant rocks
to tell of when the land was whole
before the river carved its mighty scar.

And now the river takes the easiest route,
unworried by the boulders' stubborn stance,
weaving around, forking to left and right,
letting the boulders be. The eddies dance
a celebration of this agelong truce.
The rocks remain, the river rushes past.

And boulders lend their beauty to the scene,
in greens and greys, in curves and slate-sharp planes,
their solid tones that counterpoint the trills
and grace notes of the water's sparkling song.
The river, richer far for rocks that source
the falls and pools and eddies of its course.

Diminishments

The time of our life's diminishment begins
not with the weary onset of old age,
but with our weaning, walking, talking,
learning the family's patterns.
The paradox of freedom:
choices made, options lost,
creeds solidified.
Identity.
Certainty.
Until
what?

Where now?
Who am I?
Uncertainty
is the chrysalis
which aches to break us free.
God's time. The spirit's own time
to fly free from self-absorption.
Creeds transmute from swords to ploughshares
harvesting compassion, storing wisdom
against the years of dearth. We journey inwards
to find the blazing soul within the fading frame
and returning, greet the world with a child's fresh wonder.

Jay

CALL AND RESPONSE: LECTIONARY
REFLECTIONS

A number of the poems we shared on our Poets' Corner WhatsApp were in response to the readings set for Sunday eucharists or other services, and often we sparked ideas off each other, resulting in several poems on similar themes. These poems are the result.

Emmaus Road

We journeyed westward from Jerusalem,
towards the setting sun. Our sun had set –
our blinding and enlightening sun, so warm
and rich, with soothing, gentle rays, and yet
doomed to observe its cruel, fated course
and sink beneath death's merciless horizon.
We walked and talked as we approached Emmaus,
struggling to make out any rhyme or reason
in what had passed. And then, as if a breeze
brought poignant music drifting from afar,
a strange, familiar voice beguiled our ears
with truths that soothed our misery and fear.
Our vanished sun had risen from the dead:
we knew him in the breaking of the bread.
Jay

Road to Emmaus

We walked.
Stumbling with doubt
and the bitter tang of loss
after rapt faith.
Downcast.
The dry broken road
a kiln of scorching grief.
Questions assailed us.
The hot dust choked and
the horizon shimmered,
A mirror for our confusion.
Then the stranger slipped silently between us.
Whispered:
'Peace.'
Until He broke the bread we were blind.
And yet,
with Him on that road,
the spirit swirled about us.
Opened our ears,
loosened our tongues.
Laughter fell from our serious lips.
My heart rose and sang
animated, ecstatic -
my soul burned.
Grief assuaged,
anger abandoned,
fear destroyed.
And thus comforted
we asked the stranger to stay
and found again the Lord.
So you, friend,
fearful and blinded,
casting,
lost;
dance in the reeling spirit,
unbound –
let your heart loose.

and never doubt
the Lord is with you
in friend and stranger,
without and within,
on every road.
Offer your bread with loving hands
and invite your guest to stay.
Merinda

Thomas come in and you will see

They always laughed and mocked at me, but warm
With care and kindly teasing in good part,
But never like this news set to transform,
The world to shifting truths that strain my heart.
The fantasy that Christ has cheated death
Alive, and speaking and himself again,
Although I saw him die on tortured breath.
So grateful that he suffered no more pain.
I'd need to grasp his robe and meet his gaze,
My hands to touch his flesh and his wounds too,
And see the force of life within him blaze,
For then my doubting heart would know it true.
'Thomas,' he said, 'come here.' And I was awed.
My humbled heart replied, my God, my Lord.
Merinda

Thomas

We were together till
the whole thing fell apart.
Together on the mountain, called
to be his chosen twelve –
the special ones, new Israel
chock full of hope;
sent out, no money in our belts,
but fire in our hearts.
Let demons quake, let lost ones flock
to see the kingdom lived, to enter in.
We dared to dream
of tyrants overthrown, of wine skins burst,
until the nightmare came
and we all fled.
We were together
through good times and ill.
Crunching on grain
plucked from the Sabbath fields
that set the high and mighty teeth on edge;
seeing the thousands fed, and hundreds healed,
and even several come back from the dead.
But there were times we feared
the leaders 'wrath, stones thrown,
or Roman power suborned;
and times of puzzlement and doubt:
'We do not know your endpoint, Lord, so how
can we know where we go?'
And then Golgotha came,
and we all fled.
No longer special,
proud to preach and heal;
apart, unnoticed in the lonely crowd.
In time we drifted back together to
the lonely upper room,
huddling together in our grief,
but torn apart by fear.

So what of me, so broken and so hurt
when told the nightmare's at an end,
the stone rolled back,
the tide of death reversed?
I cannot trust this light they say
has dawned anew, held as I am
in melancholy's grip.
I will not grasp
false hope and risk
the crushing blow
of yet more misery.
Yet there's another twist before
my tale is through.
'Peace be with you, doubting friend,
my peace, that will transcend your fear.
Now see me and believe.
These wounds endured for you
are yours to touch
and comprehend.'
The scales fall from my eyes.
I do not need to touch the scars
to grasp the truth and hail
my Lord and my God.
Jay

The Risen Lamb

Early
as the light sucked at the darkness
and drew the milky haze of dawn
up from the dark horizon,
the cool air let the earth breathe,
and we walked, silently, along the path
alone and together,
the mass of misery bending our weighted backs.
The myrrh and perfumes, redundant now.
We knew corruption.
For so it was in those
evil hours;
the vile court,
the trumped up charge,
lamb to the slaughter.
And then, corrupted further after death.
We had seen the sacrificial body,
and we wept.
But as we looked ahead to the hewn rock
there, sharp and glimmering,
was a light,
more brightly shining than the limpid sun of morning,
from the very shade.
The stone was simply gone,
the tomb was burst.
Frightened, I ran
in dizzying patterns around the rocks.
The thin breeze hammered in my ears.
Crazy with loss,
I left them behind
roaming into a garden.
In my desolation,
desperate with injustice,
I looked with tear blind eyes,
and cried out for him.
'Lord, oh my Lord, where have they put you?'

Softly, lovingly,
under the lamb's tender breath, 'Mary.'
Merinda

A stranger, cooking on the beach

Rough hewn, from heaving years,
glistening with slick spray,
Our tired limbs toiled,
working undirected, mute, through motions
long ingrained,
thoughts thick, lips grimly sealed against the grime.
No meeting eyes, no stirring songs,
no rhythm to our work, even
the rolling of the waves a faltering heart.
Just empty faces, empty minds and empty nets.
The rough hewn waves sustained us
through the penetrating night,
our dark souls lost,
minds concentred on our stance,
our solid legs, knees locked,
bracing us against
the bracing wind.
This nightly practice, for we still must eat,
we still must live, we still must work
our frightened families to support,
the rocking boat a shocking
instability.
The creaking planks, the cracking ropes
the shattered soundtrack to
our shipwrecked lives.
All fruitless, empty-handed.
Daybreak, a fire, a light.
A stranger, cooking on the beach,
(Where had he got his fish?)
Offering a layman's lame advice
(Who did he think he was?)
'Oh, try the other side!' Well,
that will work!
We haven't tried that yet!
We haven't plied the whole wide lake,
we haven't ploughed the furrow
of every heaving wave.

Our vanquished voices
croaking with contempt.
His humour unimpaired, as if
he'd handled hecklers before,
his stature undiminished, his command insistent,
'Try!'
And now, bursting the bonds, breaking the nets,
swamping our souls and staggering our feet,
in rushed the bounty of the dawn.
Half drowning, laughing,
all embracing, arms supporting,
now,
one thought in our erupting minds,
one hope within our heaving hearts,
the rough hewn, empty tomb.
With new strength in our thighs
we strode the surf,
reborn with every ebb and flow,
towards the shore.
Julie

Letting go

'Don't cling to me,' he said – hard words – 'for I
have not ascended to my Father yet.'
Was this a censure from her Rabboni
that took the edge of joy from her bruised heart,
or was it said affectionately? Did
he smile, and gently show her how to face
the aching sorrows of the days ahead,
to journey onward without his embrace?
It can be hard to let go of the now,
to trust that, like the lilies of the field
our naked spirits will be clothed anew,
that like the birds, we will be fed, and filled
with fire and spirit from the Holy Dove,
today's safe comforts dwarfed by future love.
Jay

Easter Morning sonnet

As the early light sucked at the darkness,
drew the milky streaks of dawn from the earth
we walked together in silent distress,
weighed and bent by the remembrance of death.
We carried spices, and the herbs to mask
decay, of my beloved, perfect, Lord,
taken and killed by those who did not ask
why they were silencing the son of God.
But then, the tomb was burst: the stone was gone.
The watchers said he was no longer there.
So through the garden desolate I ran
with crazy steps of misery and fear.
I cried, 'They've stolen you, where are you laid?'
'Mary,' he answered, 'do not be afraid.'

Merinda

Ascension Prayer

What I remember was the loss, and not
the way he left - we hardly noticed how.
The sun, it blinded us more than it ought,
stole him from sight into the drifting cloud.
We felt so brave when he was at our side,
there in the upper room and by the shore
he promised us his spirit as our guide
to keep us safe from harm forevermore.
But now this parting brought us misery,
fresh shattered dreams, with our messiah gone.
We cried for him, because we knew we'd be
bereft, and weak and finally alone.
O holy spirit, comforter and friend
come to us soon, our grieving hearts to mend.
Merinda

Barsabbas (Acts 1:23-26)

*This piece of nonsense was in response to Merinda's comment on the WhatsApp:
'I was talking earlier with someone who mentioned the poor guy who didn't get
chosen - Joseph Barsabbas called Justus. They suggested a book of the nearly folk
- James and John's other brother who was off visiting friends; the tax collector who
couldn't climb trees etc.' We only include this limerick because it prompted a more
serious effort from Merinda.*

There once was a man named Barsabbas,
(Whom please don't confuse with Barabbas),
The lot fell on Matt,
So for Joe that was that,
Which is all that we know of Barsabbas.

Jay

Response to Barsabbas: Joseph Justus

Among the crowded followers at prayer
gathered together in the upper room,
Peter 'the Rock' asked each one to compare,
two willing, wise believers, each of whom
could take the sacred duty in their hands –
to lead, to teach, to pray, and to embrace
the risk of death apostleship demands.
So who would take the traitor's vacant place?
The spirit said Matthias was the one.
But Joseph Justus, lost to history,
still with the spirit's urging, would become
a bishop to fulfil his destiny.
The grace of God apportioned each their part,
for neither was forgotten in God's heart.

Merinda

Pentecost

We were at peace, quite calm and confident:
he'd told us, 'Wait!' and so we did;
in that familiar room we'd lounge and share
our memories. What happy accident
had first drawn that man in? What incident
had touched that woman's heart and made her care
enough to help provide for us? So there
we were, at peace, and calm and confident.
Until the wind blew in. No cooling zephyr –
incinerating blast of dragon fire –
sirocco searing through complacency,
souls ablaze, hearts burning with desire,
new wine, new vision, new expectancy
tongues touched with living coals, lives changed forever.

Jay

The upper room at Pentecost

The room is thankfully quite large, and yet
It feels as if the walls pulsate with fear,
And close upon us tense and cross and het
In shouting silence, dread and dark and drear.
We lost our Christ, our teacher and our friend.
We were accustomed to his loving touch
And in this room we feared it was the end -
Our faltering faith did not amount to much,
Although we hoped that God would give us sign.
We shook our heads with doubt and human ken,
And knew our time with Him was so divine
It shouldn't be a shock it had to end.
Then rushed the wind that pushed the walls apart
And Christ in spirit burst into our heart.
Merinda

The Man (Mark 7:31-37)

I was afraid to go towards the man
and yet they pushed me, held me by my coat
and took the choice away. So it began:
my clanging tongue and strangled babbling throat
with ugly squarks and thin imagined speech
that made no sense without the sign of hands.
And yet he smiled and understanding each
vague ululation, heard my weak demands
to bless me as I am, not cause me pain.
He drew me to himself, and then aside
and spitting put his mark on me, profane,
and to my ears his burning hands applied.
Then roaring sound rushed in and so I heard
myself say LORD; my first coherent word.

Merinda

Annunciation

I'm here, the small and quiet voice replied,
for few would note the unassuming girl,
not confident but neither quite a child,
this maiden who had heard the angel call.
She looked into his glorious shining face:
the angel turned his handsome eyes to hers.
'Listen', he said, 'O Mary, bless'd with grace.
My message comes from God, allay your fears.
A loving mother you are called to be
to the messiah, Emmanuel of God.
Although the truth if you will so agree
is joy mixed with pain your whole life long,
committing all your life unto God's will.'
'This,' she cried, 'I willingly fulfil'.

Merinda

Response to Annunciation: Consent

a presence   a compulsion
fingertips lose their grip
on a receding, darkening future

the boundaries that define
a village girl
already narrow

shrink further   fate looms
brutal   remorseless
she is not sure

what this tightening within
means   her body
that has barely learnt to bleed

is unprepared
command or gift?
snatched from her imagined home

as craftsman's wife
mother of who knows who
village matron

bundled into a careening
jolting journey
not of her choosing

a light
brutal   blinding
she cannot see

yet
the opening   burgeoning
possibilities

the open plains
the pondering   the joy
the sword piercing her soul

does she glimpse
the dilating   brightening
tomorrow

Jay

Annunciation 2

She hummed a joyful simple happy tune,
a perfect match, for he said he would wait -
a gentle humble man although rough hewn,
a carpenter, and yet no carnal brute.

And she could stay beside the very hearth
of home that she had loved so well and long
and start to be a woman while still there,
not leaving now before full seasons grown.

But then the tiny room was filled with light.
It swirled and screamed
and all her thought laid bare,
and thus invited by the sense of grace
the angel filled the shuddering beating air.

He greeted her and bid her not to fear,
he was not there to cause her harm or care.
And yet she knew her destiny was here
and he was what her heart had waited for.

Not just a meek humility for her,
instead a call for sacrifice
and strength.
And Mariam knew whatever price there was,
that every thing she gained would be the cost.

The angel was not simply there to bless,
she knew her concord not a simple yes.

Merinda

Annunciation 3

Because my parents were gifted by God
and returned me to the safekeeping of the temple,
the familiar fluttering of heavenly wings
caused only mild surprise
as they stirred the air.

But I roused
for the blazing presence of the unexpected messenger.
An angel who spoke.

And thus I heard my call:
a new life
and fresh blessing.
A question to me from God.

The shining envoy,
with beat of time and snowy wing
ebbed away with the breeze.

And in the shimmering silence
rejoicing and resolved,
I heard my own resounding YES
echo on the empty air.

Merinda

Dust – Ash Wednesday 2022

When we are gone
History closes over us.
The traces become faint and blow away.
Love left behind blossoms,
Sadness delaying our dismissal
But
In kind time,
and cruel time,
That memory too
Goes to dust,
As the holder takes their final path
Behind you,
So finally you are out of sight
And the bloom of remembrance is theirs.
And so you gain eternal rest.
You are,
In every way,
dust.
ii
Dust swirls,
Physical,
Unceasing,
Restless,
from the founding
of the universe.
Even the meagre handful
We thought we owned embodied
Is turbulent,
Ungovernable and weak.
But the spirit
And inspiration
That is love
And wisdom
And grace
Is fluid
And diffuses
Through

The boundary between death and life
Leaving its vibrations behind,
While eternally
We are reborn
To God.
When what we own
Is not dust
But everlasting life.
Merinda

Response to Dust: What Remains

i
What remains?
What remains when
mortal remains
are dust?
Born of stardust,
to dust we come,
but what remains?
What glint of gold remains
in memories and dreams
of those whose paths we crossed,
who will themselves in time return
to dust of the earth?
ii
Ancestors
of blood or tribe
bolster wisdom,
foster grace.
Unfelt touches
nudge us on;
unheard whispers
give us pause;
unseen gazes
suffuse love.
Ripples spread
in streams of life.

iii
What is held
in heaven's hand,
sustained in being,
small as a hazelnut,
bright as a star?
What remains
in God's embrace,
when oceans rise
and empires fall,
and stars themselves
return to dust?
What treasure stored
in human flesh
is cherished, rescued,
safeguarded
in God's eternity?
Unending love,
undying light,
immortal fire.
Jay

Reflection 1: Rhythms of Grace (Written for an online Rainbow Service)

The rhythms of the moon, waxing and waning,
the rhythms of the tides: the ebb and flow,
the highs and the lows.
I was meant to be in step with these
dancing the monthly cycle of life
in step with my sisters
in time with my biological clock
all the other women trod the dance lightly
all the other women picked up the rhythms, in touch with the tempo,
the highs and the lows
the ebb and flow.
Only I was out of sync with the music of the spheres
only I kept to my own choreography of shame:
the flow unstoppable, the ebb unattainable, the arrhythmia
unbearable.
Tired and low and always drained, I kept company with outcasts.
Pushed to the edge.
Shut out from the red tent.
And yet stained always red,
my feet like lead.
Unclean, unwelcome, forcing every step
just to cling to life.
But when I clung to his hem,
for dear life, holding onto the edge
of hope, I felt a surge within me
different from the endless heavy flow,
a rhythm starting in my soul,
a beat beneath my feet,
a quickstep in my heart.
I rose from the dust. I stepped out
from my stained robes, unashamed.
I felt my instant freedom!
Years of pain fell away.
I felt His flow of Grace.
Clean, unforced and welcome,
I would be no longer shunned,

no longer hidden. I now
could join my sisters in their pattern,
join my hands with theirs, and fit my steps.
I had but glimpsed His feet
but could have sworn
they danced.

Julie

Reflection 2: the woman at the well

Married at 13, well, that was a shock. I mean, normal, really, all of my friends were, but to be torn from my home despite my mother's tears and sold like a chattel into the hands of a much older man, well! I coped. I cooked and cleaned, I did my duty. I didn't love him, not really. He was kind. But old. He died. I was lucky, I thought, to be picked up and rescued by a bright young thing, a handsome catch, a man I might love, I thought. Another man, another marriage. Until I felt the back of his hand. I coped. I ducked and dived. Survived the beatings. And eventually I ran. Ran in the night, found a new place, formed a new identity. And along came the love of my life. Dark skinned, bearded, beautiful. Swept me off my feet. Another man, another marriage. Seems he was sweeping other women off their feet, although I didn't know it. When I found him in bed with someone else, he divorced me just like that. I coped. I moved again. The rumours, the whispers followed me, but I held up my head. A brief arrangement with an asylum seeker, in desperation, for money, turned out badly. Another man, another marriage. This time I just about escaped his control with my finances intact. Still coping, still ducking and diving, still moving, I finally met someone stable. Another man, another marriage. We tried for kids. We tried a long time. Eventually I was discarded like an empty shell. I coped. I didn't move this time. I'd had enough of running. And the rumours, the whispers, always followed. Too tarnished to marry again, I found someone else who'd had the shine rubbed off him, another piece of damaged goods, and we lived in common law.

I held my head up high in town as much as I could, but the well was just too much. Too many other more respectable women, too much judging, too many whispers. Always being pushed to the back of the queue. Too much shame. And so here out in the heat of the day, at noon, at the quiet time, I meet another man.

And what a man. Not good looking, really, but such presence. And he sees me. I mean he sees ME. He talks to me like an equal, and suddenly the pair of us are discussing theology!!? And then he tells me everything I ever did.

This man looks into my eyes, and sees my shame, but it is as if it is as solid as water to him. He wades into the deep well of my heart, and understands and loves me as I have never been loved. In that brief encounter by the well, I find my courage, my strength and my resilience are valued and the sad litany of my life becomes as dry dust, ready to receive the life giving water of his grace, ready to become clay, to be moulded into who I was meant to be.

I run again this time. Run to tell the whole town. And I shake off my shame.

Julie

THE INTERIOR CASTLE

Jay had read and studied Teresa of Avila's Interior Castle *at university, but had never felt he was quite ready for it. Age, experience and the enforced solitude of lockdown persuaded him that the time had come to grapple with it again, and the following sonnet sequence was the result. This involved rereading, studying commentaries on the work, and most importantly of all, praying over the whole for substantial periods every day. He enjoyed the irony of writing a Corona sequence during the time of a Coronavirus pandemic. All of the poems were shared with Julie and Merinda on the WhatsApp chat, and they both made many, many constructive comments as well as lending encouragement to get the sequence finished. The sequence is not a direct paraphrase, but more of a journey alongside St Teresa.*

The First Chamber

At the soul's centre God chooses to dwell.
The soul is God's estate, a castle bright
as diamond, gardens nourished by a well
of living water; chambers full of light
unless a shroud of sins blocks out the sun.
Not just the mortal sins which kill the soul,
but low self-worth, or pride in what we've done,
or busyness: all keep us from our goal.
Self-knowledge heals, but self-obsession harms.
In prayer we bid those creeping sins Begone!
In praise we turn our eyes on Christ whose arms
outstretched upon the Cross beckon us on.
Repent, move on, draw back that shroud of sins;
self put aside: our pilgrimage begins.

The Second Chamber

Self put aside, our pilgrimage begins,
yet, rightly understood, self plays its part,
for here's the paradox that underpins
the whole: Lose self to find your true Self's heart.
Christ calls us on, through friends and books and prayers,
divine Good Neighbour, helping when we slip;
the devil calls us back, through anxious cares
about the cost of true discipleship.
Cast fear aside. Only remember this:
that Christ hung on the Cross to win us peace.
We don't need fancy doctrines, raptures, bliss,
just that our perseverance should increase.
Thus we continue, pace by dogged pace,
our journey on toward the throne of grace.

The Third Chamber, part 1

Our journey on toward the throne of grace
has started well. We pray; we turn our back
on obvious temptations; find a place
of calm devotion. What then do we lack?
'Sell all you have and give it to the poor,'
said Jesus to the rich young man, who turned,
distraught. And what of us? Must we do more?
We've worked so hard; we've tried; have we not spurned
those worldly sirens, money, sex and power?
Can we not let our ordered lives confess
the beauty of God's peace one quiet hour?
But is it more God wants? What if it's less –
less trust that our good faith will see us through,
less vain fixation on what we can do.

The Third Chamber part 2

Less vain fixation on what we can do
may help us see that all is by God's grace.
This chamber has its (subtle!) dangers too
that slow our progress to a snail's pace.
Complacency, dressed as humility:
'Sainthood's for others. If I aimed at it
that would be pride. I am content to be
God's humble servant, do my little bit.'
Or in a mockery of the parable,
the publican turns on the pharisee:
'How can he be so blind? He is so full
of stubborn pride: God let me help him see!'
Leave others to their own path and God's care;
only take up the cross that's yours to bear.

The Third Chamber Part 3

Only take up the cross that's yours to bear,
for that's more than enough. Dry times will come:
times when we find no comfort in our prayer,
and every spiritual sense seems numb.
God is still here, though being weaned away
from wordly consolations feels like loss;
we long to feel God's presence as we pray:
we'd all prefer God's comfort to the Cross.
Christ the physician heals the willing soul
not by dispensing rapture from above;
but deep within, his presence makes us whole,
the one, sure sign of which is growth in love.
Spurning the props that we relied upon,
in silence and in hope we journey on.

The Fourth Chamber, Part 1

In silence and in hope we journey on,
tongue-tied, unsure, beneath a foreign sky;
strangers abroad; familiar landmarks gone;
aware long-cherished rules do not apply.
What fervent prayers will lure God to our side?
What meditations make the path more clear?
What sage or saint will be our trusted guide?
What labours guarantee success? None here.
Weaned from the milk and honey of the earth,
far from the pastures green of fleeting rest,
defenceless, yielding to this strange new birth,
as helpless babes we suckle at God's breast.
This strange new world may seem as dark as night
until our eyes accustom to the light.

The Fourth Chamber, Part 2

Until our eyes accustom to the light
we wander puzzled, disconcerted, lost.
We pray in expectation of delight
and find, instead of sunshine, cold and frost.
Our sparrow minds flit here and there in quest
of some familiar branch on which to perch;
we seek some sign along the path to test
it truly leads to God for whom we search.
The only test that counts is love: begin
with Jesus' words: 'You'll know them by their fruits,'
for God sought us out first, and deep within
the seed grows secretly, and puts out shoots.
And through this process, steady, silent, slow,
our hearts' capacity to love will grow.

The Fourth Chamber, Part 3

Our hearts' capacity to love will grow,
not by our own hard labour, not by force;
a spring of living water from below,
God's Spirit in our hearts, will run its course.
God does the work; we just prepare the ground,
no longer shamed by being who we are –
the sheep that went astray but now are found,
the prodigals returning from afar.
God may grant sweetness and delight in prayer,
may calm a while for us that sparrow mind;
in garden or in desert God is there,
Christ within, beside, before, behind.
No longer strangers, now at last we stand –
deep peace, deep joy – at home in this new land.

The Fifth Chamber, Part 1

Deep joy, deep peace. At home in this new land,
where God is not a theory or a thought,
but is the sun, wind, earth, the gentle hand
that leads us on beyond what we've been taught,
unlearn yourself. Let know-how disappear.
No fine hewn doctrine, no technique, no art,
no words, no works, no icons aid us here;
only a waiting, self-forgetting heart.
And God may choose to still the restless mind,
wrap us in love a while, and hold our gaze,
and when we come back to ourselves we find
the incense of God's grace perfumes our days
with self-forgiving, calm humility;
a life more full, more fearless, and more free.

The Fifth Chamber, Part 2

'A life more full, more fearless, and more free
I offer you, beloved of my heart.
Behold, I stand and knock, open to me,
and I shall enter, never to depart.
But first, beloved, you must count the cost.
When you are one with me, then you will know
both rapture and the weeping of the lost;
your heart's capacity to love and grieve will grow,
learning to see as I do joy, and pain:
a dappled sky, a sparkling waterfall,
a child's terror, addict's ruined vein.
I see, I love, I weep, I share in all –
each laugh, each tear, each loss, each victory –
so can you bear the wound of love with me?'

The Fifth Chamber, Part 3

'So can you bear the wound of love with me?'
The question resonates. Can we accept
that now the butterfly must struggle free
from the secure cocoon in which it slept?
No turning back: we are a new creation,
imago dei, seeing with God's eyes
the soaring beauty and the devastation;
the Judas kiss, the Easter morn sunrise.
Our lives are hid with Christ, but Christ is rife
on earth, sprung from the tomb to breathe Shalom
on shattered souls; the Word who calls to life
those starved of hope, who makes this world his home.
One with our Lover now, the call to share
this healing work flows from our deepening prayer.

The Sixth Chamber, Part 1

This healing work flows from our deepening prayer
which led us out into the wilderness.
And what did we expect to find out there?
A cure for our inherent selfishness?
Freedom from human flesh's frailty?
That never was the plan. Through the dark night
a stranger wrestled with us ceaselessly,
then rose and blessed us in the morning light,
leaving us wounded, yet somehow more whole:
a dislocation of our arrogance;
pain like an arrow piercing to the soul
tipped with the healing salve of God's presence.
So limping on, at peace in this new day
as wounded healers we go on our way.

The Sixth Chamber, Part 2

As wounded healers we go on our way
one with our wounded Lord. We know that we
will not outgrow that which can lead astray –
the frailty, the sin – yet now we see
the promised land ahead, and who would stop
on Jordan's bank? No pride, no self esteem,
no fear of failure tempts us now to swap
this wound for ease, this wakening for a dream.
The past's a distant land. Those youthful deeds,
that earnest piety that would insist
on tribal shibboleths and rigid creeds,
are fading echoes, valleys in the mist.
We need new strength as onward we are led –
what will sustain us on the road ahead?

The Sixth Chamber, Part 3

What will sustain us on the road ahead
includes the general and the singular.
All drink the cup of grace, and all are fed
with Christ's own body, but peculiar
to each are blessings springing from the well
of living water deep within their being.
Some few are given visions: in her cell
Julian, shown a crucifix and seeing
the red blood trickle down, felt her heart warmed
with utmost joy. And such a vision still,
or word, or song, may spring forth fully formed
fit for the moment, potent to fulfil
God's purpose in the world, given through one
open to living union with the Son.

The Sixth Chamber, Part 4

Open to living union with the Son
whose flesh makes sacred our humanity,
we bask in grace. But not to everyone
does God grant visions, voices, ecstasy.
You have indwelt our hearts. You are the fire
that burns within to heal an aching world,
the inbreathed Spirit fuelling our desire
that justice freed may soar with wings unfurled.
You are the ostinato to our dreams,
the mode in which our swelling lifesong plays,
the gentle voice that spurs and guides our schemes,
the rainbow palette colouring our days.
Our lamp in darkness, our bright morning star:
in you we live and move, in you we are.

The Sixth Chamber, Part 5

In you we live and move, in you we are
at peace. No longer hoping desperately
to crack your code, or glimpse you from afar,
for you drew near to us, and chose to be
our brother, born of woman. Once we sought
to catch you in our meditations' net,
to lure you with our fervent prayers; we thought
to transcend flesh. Oh, how could we forget,
God beyond scale, vaster than galaxies,
you dance within the centre of each cell.
The petty scope of our philosophies
balks at this fact: somehow, you chose to dwell
among us, full of grace and truth. We cling
to you, whose passion is our ransoming.

The Sixth Chamber, Part 6

To you, whose passion is our ransoming
we turn. We need our daily bread, and it
is you; the simple joy of pondering
your fleshly, sweating, spitting life does not
grow stale. At home (at last!) within our skin
we know that we are loved. We do not need
to count the angels dancing on a pin,
or flee the world, or weaponise the creed.
And now the simple round of daily prayer
is love enfleshed, a basking in the light,
and love informs and sweetens all our care
for those we meet. Duty and joy unite;
our inner fears are quelled; ego departs;
you are our all, enthroned within our hearts.

The Seventh Chamber

You are our all, enthroned within our hearts.
The door was locked, and yet you entered in
with 'Peace be with you,' and our life now starts
and ends in you, for neither death nor sin
can separate us from your perfect love
which casts out fear. Unending unity
of spirit, as when rain falls from above
and joins the stream that flows into the sea.
All is one: our service and our prayer;
reborn into the world, which now we prize
as gift not chattel. Mary and Martha share
the labour and the love, and recognise
this way, this life, this truth we gladly tell:
at the soul's centre you, Lord, choose to dwell.

MUSING ON THE PARABLES

Having to preach a sermon on the parable of the wheat and the tares led Merinda to writing the first poem in the following sequence.

The Wheat and the Weeds

Find the tares and pull them up
or better still just burn the lot:
it seems the enemy of good
has sown the weeds to taint the food.

At best they grow around the crop
at worst they'll choke the entire plot
and cost us dear who need the grain
and ruin what we hoped to gain.

But the farmer knows we would confuse
green shoots of each, and could not choose
the certain wheat from what is not
and so destroy the total crop.

And so our farmer bids us stay –
we should not judge the plants this way
and risk destroying what is true
by rending seedlings into two
and rooting out the precious grain
that will not spring back up again.

Any weeds will be quite clear
for the farmer to cast into the fire.
Our task is but to tend them all
with loving care as they grow tall
and help them flourish, every one,
to bring the farmer's harvest home.

Merinda

The story of the sower

The hopeful farmer flings the seeds
casting far more than he needs
across the patch of open field
praying for a healthy yield.

But the field's a rocky tract
with hardened paths all dry and cracked ,
thick vines and weeds to choke and coil
and just a little fertile soil.

And so the seed it falls like rain,
but on the dry path fails to gain
purchase for roots beneath the top
and scorches before it makes a crop.

The weedy patch grows with the grain
but quickly smothers it again .
The shoots have no chance to grow stout,
the competition snuffs them out.

But those that fall on good terrain
root and sprout and then remain,
and so they ripen in the sun
until the growing time is done.

Thus the kingdom is revealed:
our hearts are rather like this field.
We might be dry or stony ground
with weeds to choke and to confound
or might be good and open land,
ready to nourish at God's command.

With generous hand our maker sows,
but we are responsible for what grows.

Merinda

The parable of the seeds

I found my birds and rocks and thorns
Not in the wide world's fields and ways
But in the Church's hallowed space
Where cares assault the one who prays.

The seeds of helpfulness I brought
Were quickly pecked and gobbled whole.
Committees, visits, groups and clubs:
Where was the time to feed my soul?

The seeds of change I hoped to sow,
For brighter worship, deepened prayer
Met rocky looks and shaking heads:
'He'll learn.' My plans took no root there.

And gently germinating shoots
Of wisdom that could feed the flock,
Were crowded out by age old spats
And voices raised in rage or shock.

And yet the whispered voice of God,
The warm suffusing light of Christ,
The living water from the font
Of life, remained amidst the rest.

In side aisles, chapels, quiet talks,
In friendships forming strong and slow,
In fellowship and service shared
My faith found ground in which to grow.

Jay

Mustard Seed

smallest seed of all
growing wide and tall and great
birds in huge branches

Merinda

Mustard Seed 1

Unannounced annunciation
  overwhelmed, terrified,
    light so bright it blinds.

How to answer, how to cope?
  A cuckoo growth within her womb,
    the future's walls closing in.

But sight adjusts to brightest light,
  unlooked-for vistas open up
    her quiet 'Yes' mothers us all.

Jay

Mustard Seed 2

Poor unhappy little man,
Kneeling down to pray;
Looking for the narrow path,
Not knowing the way.

Tried and failed to be a knight,
Captured, held in fear,
Ransomed by his father's gold,
Fell ill for a year.

One-time reveller in chief
Now spurned by all the youth;
Seeking a new Master's voice,
Seeking a new truth.

Then the voice: 'Rebuild my Church!'
Il Poverello stands:
And now the message spreads forth from
Assisi to all lands.

Jay

The land where parables come true

The land where parables come true,
where stragglers get a full day's wage,
and winos, weirdos, wastrels too
can take their place upon the stage
and sing their hearts out at the feast,
while Jesus helps the guests get drunk.

The poor have most, the rich have least,
and treasure's found in fields of junk,
the angels throw a party for
a coin retrieved, a lost sheep found,
so drop your baggage on the floor
and dance your feet into the ground.

Jay

THE CHURCHYARD POEMS

This sequence springs from time spent by Merinda in churchyards, including the beautiful grounds of St Giles' Church in Ashtead, and St Martha's on the Hill near Guildford.

Why is it

Why is it lord, that searching
I am drawn into your yards
or your cemeteries and gardens to find peace,
midst the symbols of your presence
and the sleepers underneath
while the quiet air sings gently
and my fretful cares release.
You bid me drop my world-resisting guard.
You call your invitation
as I choose a bench outside
and you find me, though I'm sure we are both meant to be inside.
Then the tender care you fold me in,
the sense of being truly known
rather than anonymous
inside the bustling noisy church
lets me know that I am not alone.
For the spirit that I breathe into my aching heart is yours,
and it comes as free as air or ocean spray,
and it feels as if this is the perfect hideaway to choose
to slake the thirst for you I cannot lose.

Merinda

Churchyard Poem: St Martha's Hill

I sit surrounded by the symbols of loss:
the cross, the weeping angel and the certainty of death.
And yet this is a far cry
from the Lord I want to see,
the risen soft untouchable messiah,
who walks awakened in the garden as he tests his quivering limbs
and attests to life beyond
the agony, the last abyss.

In gratitude look up to the skyline of the glorious countryside
with the colours, and the wisps of clouded breath,
blue meets orange in the foggy autumn air.
And I wonder at the freezing stone and iron.

Christ burst the tomb
as so the empty crosses speak.
But in this somber place,
a monument to death
I look for the Lord of everlasting life.
I feel he is somewhere here...
beyond the cutlery of death.

Merinda

Churchyard 3

I sit on the wet bench
beside the broken grave of Beatrice,
long gone and probably forgotten,
strewn with the confetti of damp leaves,
yellow, golden
and lichen on the stone.

The sun bathes the morning mist with a luminous glow.
Dew becomes frost becomes liquid again
and glistens in bulging droplets while
the light scent of damp decay above
mirrors decay below.
And yet,
the place hums with life and health
as fat birds feed:
dunnocks on red berries, robins on shining nut-brown seeds
and blackbirds singing their fortune's gratitude to the sky.
Sparrows peck upon the teeming insects
in the burgeoning grass
and thick hedgerows,
and everything in this concrete garden
is somehow green, or life-giving
and overspilling, grows
with unspoilt joy
around the tombstone outcrops
and Celtic crosses.
Around me,
all life
all nature's hope
as here
among the dead.

Merinda

Churchyard 4

The winter sun shines through the trees
and the sharp edge of the freezing air bites
my tender face.
I look down at the long grass and weeds
hiding the marble memorial.
'Hello Dad,' I say.
'Cold today, but clear.
I'm here to tidy you up a bit.'

Tears start to brim,
but I sniff them back.
It's been a long time,
years that have made the heart
fond and sad rather than tortured.

'I'm just cutting back the grass,' I say,
in the soft and gentle voice inside my mind
that I would use
for an elderly relative,
which he will be now.

And yet in my head
he is vital and young,
still talking and laughing.
He was dearly loved,
and is sorely missed.
which now I see
is what the plaque says.

Merinda

Churchyard 5

Today I am grumpy.
The rain has not held off
and the bench is wet
despite the promise of early sun
and there are people here.

They cannot share my solitude,
my heart's weight.
They are too loud,
too real.
Their anoraks are too bright,
their children too happy,
skipping, whooping,
too exuberant for this dignified place.

They plant plastic windmills
and glinting glass butterflies
in a recent mound of earth, and chatter
and laugh with their grown ups,
their voices high and shrill

The breeze shifts,
the laughter mingles with birdsong.

I sit rather stiffly
as they swarm a nearby path
and stare down
at shaded sodden grass,
urging them silently
to go away,
to find the solemnity
befitting the monuments.

Then she arrives
humming and trusting.
The shadow flickers.
I look up
into laughing guileless eyes.

The much-too-close child speaks:
'This is my granny's garden,'
she says, pointing.
'And we have planted her over there.'

Abruptly I feel the air defrost.
The warmth and light,
deliberately avoided,
now glowing inside.
My leaden heart lifts and begins to soar,
unsteady on new wings.
I smile uncertainly,
my gloom in tatters.
I rise to my feet
and look over her head
at the fresh grave
bright with toys.
A message in flowers
says Love.
'Show me,' I say.

Merinda

Churchyard 6

Today the children's garden at the catholic church.
Nobody here.
No bodies at all.
Blue muscari and the daffodils,
in place of graves.
The long grass grows
lush and neglected.
But not deserted:
Jesus on his cross
looks down.
Beneath his feet a tiny bed of snowdrops, windflowers, primroses...
Each one is a child not born or lost.
Nature remembers
what others dismiss,
with cowslips and pink campion.
Each one precious,
placed into God's hands,
recalled at God's feet,
blooming year on year,
herb robert, lady's smock,
forget-me-nots...
eternal life.

Merinda

Response to Why is it

Within the church the pious stand
and sing their hymns of praise.
The words inspire, the music's grand,
the organ sweetly plays.

Embroidered vestments starched and bright
adorn the solemn priest,
and stained-glass Saints suffuse the light
that streams in from the east.

The perfect liturgy glides on
with never a hitch or lag,
and no-one twigs that God has gone –
she's nipped out for a fag!

Jay

EPILOGUE

Merinda wrote this poem in May 2020, inspired by a sermon preached (over zoom) by the priest in charge of a church we all have connections with. Under Julie's leadership we regularly play together as a music group leading worship, with various other folk joining us from time to time. During lockdown we recorded a good number of songs and hymns for use in live streamed services, and called ourselves The Ragtag Minstrels. Merinda said at the time that of all the strays that she had in mind, perhaps it was most about our little ragtag group. It seems a fitting poem to end with.

Jesus' Call

What we had in common, was Jesus' call
and in the seasons of our wanderings met;
not all at once but gradually, yet all
could recognise their capture in the net
that fishes for the so peculiar soul.
Chosen, in spite of what we lacked –
we always were the outcasts from the shoal;
longing for God to usher us to act,
yearning to be journeying less alone.
But now are we made purposeful through grace,
as here we stand, drawn to the cornerstone;
a gathering of strays that found their place.
a band of minstrels all hoping to make
life-changing music, all for Jesus sake.
Merinda

ABOUT THE AUTHORS

Jay has been writing poetry since he was 12, and finds it wonderfully therapeutic along with bread-making, choral singing, walking and going to folk gigs. As a card-carrying introvert, he rather guiltily enjoyed sitting in the garden, listening to the birds, gazing at the flowers and marvelling at the vastly beautiful clear skies of the Spring and Summer of 2020. Lockdown meant crash-courses in video-editing, video-conferencing and social media streaming, but now he is glad to be back passing the time with friends in coffee shops and pubs.

Having retired once, lockdown arrived at just the right moment in time to offer Merinda some longed for space, for poetry, art, philosophy, sourdough breadmaking, food preservation, prayer, sacred listening, gardening, composing, singing, drumming, preaching, bird-watching, fendersmithing and writing - recreations that had previously been subsumed by a career in the service of child education. Now 'unlocked' she realises she needs to retire again to try the next set of exciting creative projects...

Julie is a Head of Music, multi-instrumentalist conductor, composer, performer and award-winning gardener. When the three of us (often with other friends) join together to perform as the Ragtag Minstrels, or as part of the band for Rainbow services, she is our director, and sometimes composer and arranger as well. She loves turning her hand to various arts and crafts, as her beautifully decorated home attests.

Printed by Amazon Italia Logistica S.r.l.
Torrazza Piemonte (TO), Italy

40655731R00057